Kilimanjaro

Margaret Johnson

Series Editors:
Rob Waring and Sue Leather
Series Story Consultant: Julian Thomlinson
Story Editor: Sue Leather

 NATIONAL GEOGRAPHIC LEARNING

 CENGAGE Learning·

Australia • Brazil • Japan • Korea • Mexico • Singapore • Spain • United Kingdom • United States

Page Turners Reading Library

Kilimanjaro

Margaret Johnson

Publisher: Andrew Robinson

Executive Editor: Sean Bermingham

Senior Development Editor:
Derek Mackrell

Associate Development Editor:
Sarah Tan

Editorial Assistant: Vivian Chua

Director of Global Marketing:
Ian Martin

Senior Content Project Manager:
Tan Jin Hock

Manufacturing Planner:
Mary Beth Hennebury

Contributor: Jessie Chew

Layout Design and Illustrations:
Redbean Design Pte Ltd

Cover Illustration: Eric Foenander

Photo Credits:
80 Graeme Shannon/Shutterstock
82 Roberto Caucino/Shutterstock

ISBN-13: 978-1-4240-4875-5

ISBN-10: 1-4240-4875-3

National Geographic Learning
20 Channel Center Street
Boston, Massachusetts 02210
USA

Cengage Learning is a leading provider of customized learning solutions with office locations around the globe, including Singapore, the United Kingdom, Australia, Mexico, Brazil, and Japan. Locate your local office at:
international.cengage.com/region

Cengage Learning products are represented in Canada by Nelson Education, Ltd.

Visit National Geographic Learning online at
NGL.Cengage.com

Visit our corporate website at
www.cengage.com

Printed in the United States of America
1 2 3 4 5 6 7 – 17 16 15 14 13

Contents

Review

Background Reading

People in the story

Alison
an artist and art teacher
in her mid-20s

Kelly
a history teacher

Bill
a bakery teacher

Matt
a sports teacher

Harvey
an attractive tour member
in his mid-30s

Gunter
the tour leader

The story is set on Mount Kilimanjaro, a mountain in Africa.

Chapter 1

Meeting the mountain

Take a look at this photograph. It's of me, Bill, Matt, and Kelly at the restaurant in Arusha, Tanzania, the night before we began to climb Mount Kilimanjaro. Bill asked a waiter to take it for us.

That's me, the serious-looking one. I was tired after the seven-hour bus ride from the airport. The road was full of holes and the bus was full of loud, excited talking. I sat in a corner and looked out of the window. I wanted to see the mountain.

And suddenly, after several hours, I did.

Kilimanjaro. It was just coming out from behind the clouds, and it was big, very big. I had never seen anything so beautiful in all my life and I couldn't stop staring at it. I didn't know anything then about the dangers I would face on the mountain. About how I was going to suffer, or about the big decisions I would have to make. I suppose not knowing can be a good thing sometimes, because if I'd known about all of that, then maybe I wouldn't even have gotten off the bus.

Bill was sitting next to me on the bus. "Look!" he said, pointing. "There's Kilimanjaro! Looks like an ice cream cone with all that snow on top, doesn't it?"

As he laughed at his own joke, the clouds came over and the mountain was gone.

"How do you feel about starting the climb tomorrow, Alison?"

he asked me in the restaurant later, pointing his video camera at me. He was making a film of our challenge.

I had a mouthful of food and I finished eating it before answering. "I'm looking forward to it," I said.

Bill had already finished his meal. "How do you think Gill would feel about what we're doing?" he wanted to know.

When he mentioned Gill, I put my knife and fork down.

Gill. She was my best friend. Always smiling. Always helping. Making me laugh when I was sad. Warm and loving. I knew if I tried to speak, I would start to cry.

Gill was our colleague and friend. She died early on a Sunday morning in November.

I had lunch with her at work on the Friday before it happened. She was laughing and happy, talking to me about a family party for her birthday. Then on the Monday after the party there was a phone call to the office. Gill had died in her sleep after the party. She had something wrong with her heart that nobody knew about. One moment she was there, full of life, her eyes bright as she talked about the dress she was going to wear to the party. "It's a bit too tight! Better not eat anything tomorrow!"

Then she was gone. And that wasn't all. After Gill died so suddenly like that, her daughter Susie had tests done. She found out she had the same heart problem as Gill. That's why we were here.

"Let the girl finish her food," Matt said loudly, interrupting my thoughts and speaking with his own mouth full. "She's too thin as it is! She'll need all her strength if she's going to get to the top! Alison isn't like you, Bill, eating cakes all the time!"

My face went red, but thankfully Bill turned the camera off. "I teach people to make bread and cakes," he reminded Matt with a smile. "I have to taste what they make to see if it's all right!"

As Matt laughed, he showed the food in his mouth. I saw Kelly look away from him. "Honestly, Matt," she said. "My son has better manners than you do!"

Matt smiled, not at all bothered. "Oh yes," he said. "Your son. How *is* he? It must be at least five minutes since you've spoken about him."

Kelly looked at him coldly. "You're not a family man, Matt," she said. "So you wouldn't understand. My Timothy has a lot of health problems. It's natural for a mother to worry." Her face looked troubled.

"He'll be OK, Kelly, don't worry," Bill said kindly. "Your mum's with him, isn't she?"

"Well, yes, but you didn't hear him on the phone earlier. He said he was missing me." Kelly sounded as if she wanted to cry.

"Maybe you shouldn't have come on this trip if you're so worried about him," Matt said.

I don't *think* he meant to be unkind. That's just what Matt's like. He doesn't always think before he speaks.

"I wanted to come. Gill was always a really good friend to me," Kelly said. "But that doesn't mean it's easy being away from my family." Just as she finished speaking, her phone began to ring again. "It's Timothy," she said and moved away to answer it.

"I'm pleased you're the one sharing a tent with her, Alison!" Matt laughed. "All her phone calls to Timothy would really annoy me!"

I knew what Matt meant, and to be honest, I wished I weren't sharing a tent with Kelly on this trip. We were so different. I didn't really know her very well—or Matt or Bill either. We were all colleagues, not friends; we just worked together. How was I going to manage being so close to them on the highest mountain in Africa?

But I said, "It's only for a week." As I answered, I noticed a dark-haired man sitting alone at a nearby table. I wondered if he was on our trip.

"Yes, but it's going to be the hardest week of your life so far," Matt was saying. "I don't think any of you have prepared properly for this."

"We went on all the training weekends," Bill pointed out. "We'll be fine."

Matt laughed. "You think those will be enough? None of the mountains in the UK are high enough to really get you ready for what we're going to be facing."

The dark-haired man looked up and noticed I was looking at him. I looked away quickly, afraid I had been staring. Matt looked at me. "What's wrong?" he asked, but before I could answer, the man came over to our table. "Hi, I'm Harvey," he said. "I'm part of your group. May I join you?"

Bill and Matt both looked surprised, but Bill said, "Yes, of course," and Harvey sat down. He smiled round at all of us, then he asked, "So, where are you all from?"

"Nottingham," Bill answered. "We all work in a college of further education. I'm Bill, I teach bakery, that's Matt, he teaches sports, and Alison, art. Oh, and that's Kelly over there, on the phone. She teaches history."

"A table of teachers!" Harvey said brightly. He looked about thirty-five, and he had a nice smile.

"What do you do?" Bill asked Harvey.

"I'm an engineer," Harvey said. "When I'm not traveling."

"Do you travel a lot then?" Bill asked.

Harvey smiled. "As much as possible," he said. "I've been all over the world. This is my third time in Africa." Then he looked at Matt. "Have we met before?" he asked. "Your face looks familiar."

"I don't think so," Matt said coldly.

"Matt used to play rugby for England," Bill told Harvey. "Perhaps you recognize him from those days."

Harvey was still looking at Matt. "Yes, of course," he said. "Didn't you have to stop playing because you hurt your leg?"

"That's right," said Matt unhappily.

There was a difficult silence. Then Kelly came back to the table.

"Timothy's not at all well," she started to say, then she noticed Harvey. "Oh!" she said. "Hello!"

"I'm Harvey," Harvey smiled. "I've just been learning about all of you."

Kelly sat down. "Oh," she said. "So you know about Gill and her daughter?"

No! I thought. *Don't tell him about Gill and Susie. They're ours!*

But it was too late. Harvey was looking round at us, interested. "No," he said. "Not yet. Who are Gill and Susie?"

So I had to sit and listen while Bill and Kelly told Harvey the whole story.

"Gill was the college counselor," Kelly finished by saying.

"She really helped me when my marriage broke up."

"She was funny," Bill said. "She could always make you laugh when you were feeling down."

Like me, Matt didn't say anything, but I knew he'd often spoken to Gill. I think she helped him a lot after he was told he would never be able to play sports professionally again. It was hard for him to accept that his career as an international sportsman was over.

I hadn't said anything to Harvey yet. Now I could feel his eyes on me, wondering why I was so quiet. "We're climbing Kilimanjaro to raise money for Gill's daughter Susie. She needs to have an operation," I told him. "Her best chance is to go to America for it."

Harvey nodded. "That's a very big reason to get to the top," he said. Then he added, "I'm afraid my reasons for being here are a bit more selfish than yours. Oh, I'm raising money for a good cause like everyone else, but I'm mainly here because I love a challenge. And what better challenge is there than climbing the highest mountain in Africa?"

The highest mountain in Africa. Suddenly it all seemed very real and I felt quite afraid. If all four of us got to the summit, then a local business was going to give us most of the money for Susie's operation. But what if Matt was right and the climb was too much for me? What if I were the one who failed Susie?

Chapter 2

Starting to climb

I couldn't eat much breakfast the next morning. I'd been lying awake most of the night thinking about the climb and now I wanted to get started. We all had to have our bags weighed to make sure they weren't too heavy. That took quite a long time, but finally we were ready to go. With twenty of us in the bus and everyone talking excitedly, it was really noisy again.

Then at last, we arrived at the Lemosho Gate at the bottom of Mount Kilimanjaro. And Gunter, our tour leader, introduced us to our guides and to the porters, the people who were going to carry all our bags, equipment, and supplies up the mountain. I couldn't believe how many of them there were. Now we were a *really* big group!

So many people. So much noise. "It's just like a party!" laughed Bill. "Perhaps we should dance up the mountain!"

"I think you should just think about putting one foot in front of the other," Matt said.

We waited in line to sign our names in the visitors' book. I could see Harvey in front of me. He was talking to an older couple. Then at last we set off, carrying our lunch, water bottles, and raincoats in our backpacks. We were a large, and suddenly very quiet group.

Bill made another joke. "Are we there yet?" he asked. Most people nearby laughed, and so did Bill, pleased to be the center of attention.

I let them all go ahead and found myself near the back where I hoped I could find some peace and quiet. I wanted to really take in the sights and smells of Africa.

Africa. I wasn't like Harvey, traveling to different countries all the time. I'd only been overseas once in my life so far, and that had only been to Europe. I'd always wanted to travel, and now here I was, thousands of miles from home. For a moment I allowed myself to not think about the reason I had come here; I just tried to enjoy the moment.

We were walking through a rain forest. Everything was very green. The smell of the earth and the leaves was amazing. I could hear monkeys somewhere ahead. It was all so foreign and exciting that I forgot about all the people. I thought instead about how I could paint everything I was seeing.

"Are you OK?" It was Gunter, our tour leader, checking up on me. I realized I was right at the back of the group.

"Sorry," I said. "Do you want me to walk faster?"

"No, not at all," Gunter told me with a smile. "It's best not to walk too fast at these heights. People who do so often get altitude sickness. Just so long as you're feeling OK."

I smiled at him. "Yes, I'm fine, thanks," I said, though actually the path was a lot harder than I had expected it would be. I had thought the climb would start off easily, but the backs of my legs were already really burning from the effort of walking up.

I didn't mention this to Gunter though. After all, this was Day One, and things were only going to get harder. "I was just . . . you know, taking it all in," I said. "I'm an artist. Well, an art teacher. I want to do some paintings of the trip when I get back."

Then suddenly, just as Gunter was about to reply, there was a noise behind us. "Porters!" called Gunter to everyone. "Step to the side please!"

I moved over to the side of the path and watched, open-mouthed, as a long line of porters almost ran past us. All of them were loaded up with bags, tents, or food. I could see my own bag balanced on somebody's head. None of the porters was out of breath. It was an amazing sight.

When we started walking again, I saw that Matt was walking quickly ahead, trying to catch up with Harvey and the other leaders.

Gunter didn't look too pleased. "He's walking too fast," he said. "He could get altitude sickness that way. Excuse me, Alison."

"Yes," I said, "of course." And Gunter walked on.

A little later, I found Bill waiting for me. He had his video camera pointing my way. I smiled, though I didn't really feel like it. "Did you see those porters?" he asked.

"They were a bit difficult to miss," I said and I wondered if he were finding the walk as difficult as I was.

Bill laughed. "They were, weren't they? I thought about asking them if they'd carry me up. Hard work, isn't it? My legs are hurting. Don't tell Matt I said so though, will you? He's certain I'm not going to make it to the top. I told him that if I can teach a class of twenty teenagers to bake perfect bread, then I can climb a mountain for a friend."

Bill stayed with me for the rest of the day's walk. He didn't look very fit, but he still managed to talk all the time while he was walking. I was tired after not sleeping well the night before and I began to get a headache.

By the time we arrived at our first camp, I was hot and very tired, and it didn't improve my mood when I saw Matt waiting for us with a huge smile on his face. "What took you so long?" he asked Bill. "Been baking bread on your way up?"

"Ha, ha," said Bill. Then Matt looked at me. "Dave always says you take ages to do anything, Alison," he joked. "Guess he's right!"

He was talking about David Spence, the Head of Art at the college. I had to work with the man, but I didn't like him much. He was always pushing me around. I knew he and Matt were great friends, but I felt angry that David must have talked about me to Matt.

"Oh dear," Matt said, looking at my face and laughing. "Something tells me I'm not very popular around here. Come on, Bill, I'll show you where our tent is. You look as if you need to lie down."

Matt led Bill to their tent, and I watched them go, still feeling angry about Matt's comment. What did David Spence mean by saying I took ages to do anything? It wasn't true!

Kelly put her head out of the tent next door to Matt and Bill's. When she saw me she waved. I went over, really hoping she wouldn't feel like talking. I just needed to lie down and relax for ten minutes. If I *could* relax after what Matt had just said.

"I don't think dinner will be long," Kelly said brightly when I arrived. "I think they're going to bring us some water to wash with soon. I could do with a wash, I don't know about you. It was so hot today, wasn't it? It's hard to believe we'll be walking through snow in a few days' time!"

Like Bill, Kelly didn't seem to need me to answer her, so I just let her talk, lying back on my sleeping bag and closing my eyes. I hoped that when she saw me with my eyes closed she would realize I wanted to rest, but she didn't. "I'm just going to call home," she said and started searching in her bag for her phone.

I could hear Bill and Matt laughing about something in the tent next door. Was Matt telling Bill about something else David Spence had said about me?

Kelly was still looking for her phone. "Now where is it? I know it's in here somewhere!"

A picture of David Spence rose up behind my closed eyes. He wasn't looking happy, but that wasn't unusual. He rarely did when he looked at me. I never seemed to be able to do anything right as far as he was concerned. My classes were too noisy or too quiet. My students weren't making enough progress. I didn't put enough time into my planning. And now I always took a long time to get things done! The man was just impossible to please.

How often had I complained to Gill about him? A lot. She had always listened and offered me advice. But she wasn't around to advise me anymore, and knowing that made me feel really empty and alone.

"Oh, no, I don't believe it!" Kelly said. I looked over and saw that she had found her phone at last. "There's no phone connection!"

I had to hide my smile. Maybe now I could have a little peace and quiet!

Chapter 3

Too much company

Dinner was in a big tent called the food tent. I waited a few minutes to go in after we were called. I still felt like being quiet and I was hoping to avoid sitting with the others.

When I went in, Bill, Matt, and Kelly were in deep conversation about something. They didn't see me so I sat alone.

As I sat down, a few people smiled a welcome at me. They probably would have spoken too, but after I'd smiled back, I got out my sketchbook and pen and began to make some notes and quick drawings. I wanted to record my impressions of the day to help me with my paintings when I got home.

But then Harvey came and sat down in the chair opposite.

"Good evening, everyone," he said in a confident voice. Then he smiled at me. "Hello again, Alison."

"Hi, Harvey," I said.

"I hear we've got fish for dinner," he said. "Two thousand eight hundred meters up a mountain and they manage to cook fish for us. I think that's impressive."

The man sitting on Harvey's left began to talk to him, and I tried to go back to my sketchbook, but I couldn't concentrate. Harvey was describing other trips he had been on in Africa, and what he was saying was interesting.

Our food arrived. Harvey had been right about the fish. It came with vegetables and rice and it was very tasty.

"So, you're not sitting with your friends tonight then, Alison?" Harvey observed. "Are you feeling in need of a break from them already?"

I wasn't sure how to answer that. After all, it was true: I *did* feel I needed a break. But I knew it wouldn't sound very good if I said that out loud.

So instead I just said, "It's been a long day."

Harvey smiled at me. "You picked the wrong trip if you like to be alone," he said. "Apart from the fact that there are a lot of people in this group."

"Yes," I couldn't help saying, "I *had* noticed that, actually!"

Harvey smiled again, then continued. "Unless you're very fit and very experienced, you need to attempt this kind of thing as part of a team, supporting and encouraging each other."

That made me feel a bit angry. I don't know why; it was exactly the kind of thing Gill would have said to me. But Gill had been a friend and this man was a stranger. "Who are *you* here with then?" I asked.

Harvey smiled again. "Me?" he said. "I'm here alone. But then I know what I'm doing."

The man to Harvey's right said something to him, so that was the end of our conversation, which was probably a good thing.

The meal was almost over. As we started to clear our plates, Gunter got to his feet to talk to us about the next day. "I suggest you all get to bed early so you feel rested for tomorrow," he finished off.

I pushed my chair back and stood up. Harvey looked in my direction. "I hope you aren't angry with me?" he asked. "I'm sorry. I'm afraid I usually say what I think. It isn't always a good thing."

He smiled up at me, and his smile was really pleasant. I wanted to stay angry with him, but I couldn't. "No," I said. "I'm not angry."

Anyway, I knew he was right. Because of what we were trying to do for Susie, we were a team, the four of us —me, Bill, Kelly, and Matt. And if we were going to be a successful team, then I probably did need to try to be friendlier toward them. The trouble was, I'd always been quite a private person, and ever since Gill's death I'd moved away from people even more than usual. I was sad and hurting and I suppose I just didn't want people to know how much.

"Good," Harvey smiled. "I'm pleased we're still friends. See you tomorrow, Alison. Sleep well." Then he left.

Bill, Matt, and Kelly were still sitting at the table. I decided to start being friendlier right away, and I went over to them.

"Hello, Alison!" said Bill brightly. "We were wondering where you'd gone!"

Matt wasn't so welcoming. "Alison obviously prefers Harvey's company to ours," he said.

"I'm not surprised!" said Kelly. "Harvey is a very attractive man!"

"Alison is also single," Bill pointed out. "So why not?"

Hey! I wanted to say. *I am here, you know, while you're busy discussing me!*

But Matt hadn't finished. "I thought we were here to raise money for Susie, not to find a life partner!" he said.

Life partner! I was very pleased Harvey hadn't been around to hear that one!

"It's not like that," I said. "Harvey's just a friendly guy!"

"Oh, yes," laughed Matt, obviously not believing me, and suddenly all my good intentions to be friendlier flew away into the night air.

"Anyway, I just came over to say goodnight," I said. "I'm going to bed." And I walked away.

"You shouldn't let Matt annoy you," Kelly advised a short while later in our tent. "He just likes a joke."

"Yes," I agreed. "But his jokes aren't usually funny." I was trying to take my clothes off in the small space. It wasn't at all easy.

"It's just his way," Kelly went on.

She was looking for something in her bag. Her phone, probably. As she moved things about, her water bottle fell out. It landed on my sleeping bag and the top came off. Water went everywhere. Now I had a wet sleeping bag.

"Oh no!" cried Kelly. "Alison, I am *so* sorry!"

"It's OK," I said, putting my teeth together to stop from screaming.

But Kelly was still worried. "Perhaps you better have my sleeping bag?" she suggested.

"No, thank you," I said. "I'll be fine." Then I got into my wet sleeping bag and turned on my side away from her.

It was going to be a long night.

Chapter 4

Altitude

Two hours after we started walking the next day, we came out of the rain forest and into a country of rocks and plants. It was wild, with a strange beauty that I found really exciting. If only I wasn't finding the walk so hard, I would have enjoyed it even more.

I'd always known that climbing Kilimanjaro was going to be a challenge, but I had expected to be able to take pleasure from the views. That morning, though, it was taking almost all my energy just to walk.

"Isn't this great?" Bill said, joining me. "It looks like a movie set up here! I bet you'd like to paint all of this." He was filming everything as he spoke, and he was so bright and happy I couldn't stand it.

"Aren't you tired?" I asked him.

"Not really," he said. "I slept very well last night."

I had heard him. *And* Matt.

Bill saw my face. He laughed. "Oh, dear!" he said. "Were we both snoring?"

"Yes," I said. "You were a bit."

"Sorry about that," Bill said.

Soon after this, I needed to go to the bathroom. "Excuse me," I said to Bill.

Bill laughed and waved his hands towards the plants.

"Choose carefully," he joked. "Some of the bathrooms around here look as if they have sharp leaves."

Thankfully, when I came out from my plant bathroom a little while later, Bill had gone farther up the mountain. A few of the guides had waited for me a respectful distance away, and I saw that someone else was waiting with them—Harvey.

"Still being unfriendly?" Harvey joked as we began to walk together.

There he went again! "Do you always think the worst of people?" I responded.

"Not if they prove me wrong," Harvey said. "But every time I look at you, you have this great big 'keep away from me' look on your face."

"And you have a great big 'I'm always right' look on yours!" I told him angrily. I don't know why, but somehow I was able to say what I thought with Harvey.

I could tell he didn't mind, because he laughed out loud. I smiled too. I couldn't help it.

"Well that comes from the fact that I *am* right the majority of the time!" he said. Then he asked how I'd slept the previous night so I told him about the snoring and the water bottle accident. But he wasn't very impressed. "That's just what life's like when you're with other people, Alison," he said. "I'm guessing you live alone and you're not used to it, right?"

I wished he were wrong, but he wasn't. "I do live on my own," I admitted. "Don't you then?"

Harvey shook his head. "No, I have students living with me. The money they pay me for their rooms helps me to come on trips like this. And they're good company, too."

We walked silently for a moment. It was very hot and still. I imagined Harvey and his students in a big kitchen cooking a meal together. They would want to hear about his travels. He would be an interesting person to share a house with. Unless you wanted to spend any time on your own, that was!

"What about you?" Harvey asked. "What sort of place do you live in?"

We were going up a steep hill. I had to wait a moment to get my breath. "I only have a small apartment at the moment," I answered at last. "But I should be moving soon. My dad's offered to help me so I can get some money from the bank to buy a house."

"Great," Harvey said. "Good old dad!"

"Yes," I agreed.

"Where will you buy?" Harvey wanted to know.

"Close to where I work in North Nottingham, I suppose," I answered. "Dad only made me the offer last week, and because of this trip, I haven't had much chance to think about it."

"I used to visit Nottingham quite often," Harvey surprised me by saying. "I had a friend who lived there for a few years. Isn't North Nottingham a bit of a rough area?"

"I like it," I said, but as I spoke, I wondered whether Dad would be happy about me buying a house there.

I hadn't *asked* my dad for help. In fact, I hadn't even thought about buying a house. But Dad really wanted me to own my own place to live. If he was putting money into it, I knew he would want to help me make my choice. I loved the area around the college; people from all over the world lived there. But I was pretty sure Dad wouldn't share my opinion about it.

"I'm sure you'll find somewhere you both like," Harvey continued.

"Yes," I agreed doubtfully, but suddenly I wasn't looking forward to house hunting anymore. Dad and I would argue; I just knew it.

But just then Harvey touched my arm to show me something, and when I looked up, all thoughts about houses left my mind. "The summit!" I said as the top of the mountain came into view. "Oh, it's so beautiful! I saw it yesterday from the bus, but this is even better!"

"It's going to be extremely cold up there," Harvey warned. "I hope you packed enough warm clothing!"

I wasn't sure that I had, but I didn't plan to worry about it. The view was so wonderful that I didn't want anything to spoil it for me. Even when the clouds rolled over to hide the mountain again, the image of the summit stayed with me. I tried not to think how far away it had looked, and, when we stopped for something to eat, I took my sketchbook and a pencil from my backpack and did a little drawing of the mountain from memory.

"That's really good," Harvey told me.

A feeling of pleasure washed over me. "Thanks," I said.

Then Kelly came over to take a look. "My Timothy likes drawing," she told me.

I was aware of Harvey nearby, looking to see if I was going to be unfriendly again, so I smiled at Kelly. "Does he?" I asked. "What does he like to draw?"

So that's how I came to listen to Kelly talking about Timothy for the next hour. I was as friendly as I could possibly be. Which was why it was so funny when Kelly turned to me and said, "I'm sorry, Alison, it's been lovely talking to you, but I need to save my breath for walking now."

I hid my smile. "Yes," I agreed. "The path has become more difficult, hasn't it?"

Then, for a few wonderful minutes there was silence, except for the sound of our boots on the path and our bodies working to get enough breath.

Some large black birds flew close to us, rolling and turning through the air as if they were having a flying competition. I smiled at them with pleasure, thinking how free and easy it looked up there, high on the mountain. "They're laughing at us!" I said, but Kelly didn't look interested.

Up ahead, somebody else was laughing. Matt. He was walking with a very pretty girl, and he seemed to be finding something she was saying very funny. Clearly he found her attractive. Clearly too, Matt had forgotten about his girlfriend at home. Oh well, it was nothing to do with me.

Matt sat with the pretty girl at dinner after we arrived at Shira One Camp. I sat with Bill and Kelly; I wasn't sure where Harvey was. After the long day's walk, every part of my body was hurting. It took all my energy to keep my eyes open. I just wanted to lay my head down on the table and go to sleep.

"Look at Matt with that girl!" Bill was saying.

"Don't film him, Bill!" Kelly said. "His girlfriend might see the film!"

Their voices seemed to come from a long way away. The food arrived. It smelled very strong. Too strong. Suddenly, I knew I had to get out of the food tent as quickly as possible.

"I just need to get something from the tent," I said and then I ran.

Voices followed me. "Alison? Are you all right?" But I kept on running.

I made it to about twenty meters away from the food tent. Then I stopped and hung my head, my whole body wet with heat.

And that's when Harvey appeared.

"Alison? I saw you run out of the food tent. Are you OK?"

I didn't want him to see me being sick.

"Go away!" I said, but he wouldn't and though I tried, I couldn't control the bad feeling in my stomach. I was loudly, terribly sick. Again and again.

"That's it, let it out," said Harvey.

I felt about five years old. I wanted to die.

Harvey's hands slipped down to my shoulders. My stomach was empty. I was worn out by the effort of being sick and by the activity of the day. I remembered it was my birthday the next day and felt a bit sorry for myself. "There," said Harvey. "Feeling better now?" His voice was kind.

Suddenly Gunter was there. Someone else to see me in that state!

"Are you all right, Alison?" he asked.

Harvey answered for me. "Just a little altitude sickness," he said. "I'll help her to bed."

"Good," said Gunter. "I'll check on you in the morning. OK, Alison?"

It took every last drop of my strength to get to my tent.

"Sleep well, Alison," Harvey said as he left me in my sleeping bag.

"Good night," I said. "And . . . well, thanks."

"You're welcome," Harvey said, and left.

I went to sleep straight away, but unfortunately, I woke a few hours later. Being at a high altitude made me want to go to the bathroom more than usual, and I had to get up even though all I wanted to do was sleep.

Kelly was fast asleep, and I moved as quietly as I could so I wouldn't wake her. But it was very cold—far too cold to go outside without putting more clothes on. So I put on my coat, shoes, and hat. Every little thing I did took so long and needed so much effort. I felt as weak as a baby. I knew it was only the effects of being at high altitude, but it was still very annoying.

Finally, finally, I managed to get out of the tent. And when I did, my breath caught in my throat with amazement—because there were thousands of stars in the sky. *Millions.*

I was totally moved by the sight. And as I stood and just stared and stared, tears filled my eyes. Looking up at the black and silver night I felt very small and insignificant. The sky and its stars were so huge and impressive, and I was so lucky to be here on the side of the highest mountain in Africa, seeing this sight. Gill would have loved this so much, and I wished with all my heart that she were there next to me.

"Hi, Alison," said a voice in the dark.

Not Gill, but . . . Matt. The very last person on Earth I would have chosen to share this special moment with. He was wearing a head torch, and it hurt my eyes as he looked in my direction.

"Got a secret meeting with Harvey, have you?" he asked. His voice wasn't entirely pleasant, and I felt a bit fed up. *You're the one who's been talking to a pretty girl all day when you have a girlfriend at home!* I thought. But I didn't say anything.

"No," I said, making sure to keep my voice quiet, even though I was angry. "I just need to use the bathroom."

"Oh," said Matt. "Well, you can't miss it. Just follow your nose. It smells terrible."

And just like that, the wonderful roof of stars suddenly didn't seem to be quite so bright.

Chapter 5

Happy birthday!

The first person I saw when I left the tent the next day was Gunter.

"Good morning, Alison. How are you feeling?" he asked.

I didn't feel great, but I lied. "Fine, thanks, Gunter," I said. "Much better."

"That's good. But make sure you walk slowly today," Gunter advised. "You'll enjoy it, I think. The views from Shira Cathedral are amazing. That will give you the strength to reach the next camp."

I did my best to smile. "Let's hope so," I said and continued towards the food tent. Although I didn't feel like it, I knew I needed to eat.

I sat on my own in the food tent but Bill soon joined me. "All right this morning?" he asked. "We thought you might be feeling a bit ill when you ran out like that last night."

I didn't want to explain to him what had happened. I just wanted to sit quietly and eat my breakfast. So I said, "No, I'm fine thank you."

Kelly joined us. She was smiling happily. "Guess what?" she said. "My phone's working OK this morning! I wish there wasn't a two-hour time difference between here and the UK. Timothy will be at school now. I'll phone Mum instead."

She proceeded to do so, and, because she was missing Timothy so much, the conversation was both loud and emotional. Soon I was starting to get a headache.

Bill was talking to me about something, I don't know what. Some project he wanted to start at college. The beauty of the previous night's sky seemed very distant.

By the time Kelly had finished her phone call, I was feeling really upset. I'd been hiding how I really felt about Kelly using her phone all the time for days now, and I just couldn't do it any longer. I did my best to keep my voice calm, but I just had to speak. It was either that or blow up. "Actually, Kelly," I said, "don't you think you use your phone a bit too much? This is Africa after all, not London. We're meant to be having an adventure. If you phone home all the time, it means it's hardly any different to normal life."

Kelly stared at me. "I haven't used it that much! Only to check that Timothy's OK! He's only seven years old, you know!"

I should have stopped there, but somehow I couldn't. "Bill's son is only two, but he doesn't phone home all the time," I said.

"My wife is very able," Bill said. But his usual smile had disappeared and he was looking a bit angry with me.

"So is my mother," Kelly said. "But it's different. A young child needs his mum, and Timothy has health problems!" She sounded close to tears now, and I wished I'd never brought the subject up.

But as I had . . . "Well, I'd be really thankful if you wouldn't make all your phone calls in the tent or at the table," I said.

"We probably won't be able to use our phones when we go higher anyway!" Kelly said, and then she *really* looked as if she were going to cry.

"I'm sure it will be OK, Kelly," Bill comforted her. "Don't worry." As he put his arm around her, he gave me a cool look.

I left them to it and made my way back to the tent. As I went, I thought that Matt would really approve of what I'd just done, which made me wonder if it had been a good idea. After all, I didn't like Matt very much.

Then I reached the tent. And the minute I went inside, I felt as bad as it was possible to feel. Because someone . . . and that someone was obviously Kelly . . . had put balloons up in the tent. And a brightly colored sign that said *Happy Birthday, Alison!*

I sat down and looked at it all, feeling terrible. I thought about Kelly sitting in the tent, blowing those balloons up to give me a nice surprise. It can't have been easy at this altitude. She must have come over to the food tent feeling really excited about me finding them. Only for me to be mean about her using her phone. Why had I done it? What was the matter with me? I didn't usually complain about things like that.

I could easily picture how Gill would have looked at me if she'd still been here. "Oh, Alison!" she would have said.

I spoke to her now as if she were really there. *"All right. I'll find her and say thank you. And sorry."*

"That's OK," Kelly said tightly when I did. But she still looked upset. And Bill still wasn't looking very friendly towards me either.

"No, really," I went on. "It was a very nice thing to do for me. I can't imagine how you managed to blow them up at this altitude!"

"I brought a balloon pump to blow the balloons up," Alison said coldly, which made me feel worse than ever. She had obviously planned the balloons for me in advance, before the trip.

"Well, thanks," I said. "And I . . . well, I hope I didn't upset you just then. You know, about your phone."

"Not at all," Kelly said. "I'll make sure I don't use my phone when you're around."

I was still feeling bad when we started walking shortly after this. So when Harvey came to join me, I spoke quickly. "Don't," I said. "Just don't say it."

"Don't say what?" he asked.

"Anything about anything!"

Harvey smiled. Not for the first time, I felt he knew exactly what I was thinking. "OK, I'll leave you alone, if that's what you want," he said, "if you sit with me at dinner tonight."

Clearly he wasn't going to take no for an answer. And I wasn't sure I wanted to say no anyway. It was my birthday, after all. "All right," I agreed. "But I don't want to have my character analyzed all evening."

He gave me a big smile. "Now would I do that?"

"Er, yes . . . !" I said, but I couldn't help smiling. Then I caught sight of Kelly's unhappy-looking face and I stopped smiling.

Oh well, at least there were the amazing views from the rocks at Shira Cathedral to look forward to.

At first the walk was easy. The ground was flat, which was a nice treat, and the sun was out. I was able to look at the views and take a few photographs to help with paintings when I got home.

But then, without any warning at all, the fog came down. One moment it was sunny and the next I could hardly see the person in front of me. It wasn't at all pleasant, and I needed to concentrate very hard on where I was putting my feet. And suddenly we weren't walking on flat ground anymore.

"We're going up now, towards Shira Cathedral," Gunter told us. "Take care and take your time. It's a difficult climb."

He was right. It was difficult. *Very* difficult. My legs hurt, my heart was racing, and it was difficult to get enough breath. All the way up I was hoping that the fog would blow away so we would have the views Gunter had promised us from the top.

But the fog didn't lift, and there were no views—just a screen of cold, white fog.

I felt sad and beaten, and I know I wasn't the only one. The group was usually quite noisy, but nobody was talking much, especially when it began to rain and a wind came up, blowing the rain into our faces. I was freezing.

Then suddenly I seemed to see a face through the fog and the rain—a face lit up by happiness. Gill's face. I could hear her voice in my head so clearly it was as if she were really there, talking to me.

"Susie's got into the university she wanted! She got the letter yesterday! Isn't that great?"

And I remembered how Gill had hurried into the staff room one morning to tell me the good news. Susie was at that university now, halfway through her training to become a doctor. She would be a good doctor if she got the chance to have her operation and finish her course—I knew it. Susie was warm and kind like Gill. She was worth all of this. I had to remember that.

Looking ahead, I saw Bill and Kelly walking silently with their heads down. I wanted to go up to them to remind them why we were doing this. But after upsetting them that morning, I didn't quite have the confidence, and that made me feel bad all over again.

Oh well, at least Harvey seemed to enjoy my company.

But when I met up with Harvey later, there was something different about him. Oh, he was pretty much the same at first. He asked how the day had been for me and when I told him about my legs hurting and the fog, he said, "Gunter's a great guide, but even Gunter can't order the weather to suit us."

He was right, of course. "Why is it that whenever I speak to you I feel like a child?" I asked.

Harvey smiled. "Er . . ." he started to say, but I held up my hand.

"Don't answer that!"

Harvey laughed, but then I realized there was something different about the sound of that laugh. For some reason he just didn't seem like his usual relaxed self.

"Is everything all right?" I asked, studying his face.

"Of course," he answered quickly. "Why wouldn't it be?" Then the food was served so the subject got dropped.

As we began to eat, I remembered how I'd kept myself going that day by thoughts of Susie. I couldn't imagine being able to do something as hard as this without a personal reason like that. And Harvey didn't have that kind of a reason to be here.

So I asked, "Do you ever wish you hadn't come on this trip?"

A strange look crossed over Harvey's face. Then I noticed there were dark circles under his eyes. He looked really tired.

"Why should I wish that?" he asked.

There had been an edge to his voice, and I looked at him, surprised.

"Do *you* regret it?" he asked. "Is that why you're asking me?"

"No!" I said. I felt a bit upset by the way he was talking. "I mean, it is hard, *very* hard. But how could I regret it when we're doing this for Susie? She's Gill's daughter! And Gill . . . well, sometimes I think she's the only person who ever really understood me!"

As ever when I thought about Gill, I felt upset.

Harvey reached across the table and took my hand. I knew it was his way of saying he was sorry.

"What about your dad? Doesn't he understand you?" he asked.

"No," I said sadly, "not really. We've never gotten on that well. It was just him and me after Mum died. Oh, he loves me; he wants the best for me. But we argue a lot. He doesn't trust me to make my own decisions. Dad's the reason I went into teaching really. He didn't think being an artist was a very secure job."

I glanced up to find that Harvey wasn't looking at me.

He wasn't looking at anything really; his eyes were sort of unfocused. And he had one hand up to his head as if it were hurting.

"Harvey?" I said, and he seemed to come back into the room.

"Go on," he said. "I was listening. You didn't really want to be a teacher."

He smiled at me, so I continued. "Well, no, I didn't, not really. And I don't think I'm very good at it. The kids all give me a hard time; I don't know how to deal with them. My boss is always telling me I do things wrong, and that gives me even less confidence. Sometimes I think . . ."

But at that point, a man I'd seen Harvey speaking to before came over. "Mind if join you?" he asked.

And I was sorry to hear Harvey say, "Not at all, Geoff."

Geoff sat down and the two of them started talking.

I listened for a while as I got on with my meal. Harvey still didn't sound right to me, but Geoff didn't seem to think there was anything strange about him.

To be honest, I was feeling a bit down, wondering if Harvey had been bored with me talking about my problems. Had he been pleased that Geoff had come along when he had? I had been talking to Harvey the way I used to talk to Gill. But it was no use; Harvey *wasn't* Gill.

Chapter 6

The Barranco Wall

Kelly was just leaving the tent next morning when I woke up. I could hear the sound of rain falling. I got dressed, thinking about everything that had gone wrong the previous day. I couldn't do anything about the weather, but I could try to make peace with Kelly and Bill.

When I went into the food tent, I saw them straight away. They looked as if they were talking about something serious, and I waited for a moment, not sure how welcome I would be. Harvey was sitting at the other end of the table. For a moment I thought about going to join him, but then I seemed to hear Gill's voice in my head again. *Go on. If you don't try and make things right now, it could end up being too late!* So I went over to Bill and Kelly.

"Morning," I said.

They both looked up at me. "Morning, Alison," Kelly said quietly, and, as I watched, she put her phone away in her pocket.

"I thought I'd try to give Susie a call," she explained, "to see how she is and tell her how we're getting on. But I'll wait until after breakfast."

"It would be nice to speak to her," I said. Bill still hadn't said anything to me yet, and I just didn't know how to put things right. I knew I had to say sorry, but somehow it just didn't seem very easy to do it. "How's Timothy?" I asked Kelly instead.

It was the wrong thing to say. Bill looked up at me. "She's too scared to phone him," he told me. "She thinks she'll upset you if she does."

"It's all right, Bill," said Kelly gently, then she looked at me. "I thought about what you said, Alison, and I think you're probably right. I do worry about Timothy too much."

Matt chose that very moment to join us. "Have I come in time for the daily Timothy report?" he said. "Oh good!"

"Don't *you* start!" Bill said. "Kelly's already had Alison complaining to her about it. She doesn't need you to do it, too."

"Alison?" Matt said. "Surely she's far too busy getting friendly with Harvey to have the time to upset Kelly!"

My face went red. "It's not like that," I told him. "We're just friends."

"Oh, yeah," smiled Matt, making me feel like hitting him.

But before I could say anything else, Gunter came over. "I hope you are all feeling well this morning?" he asked.

"Absolutely great!" Matt answered for all of us.

Gunter smiled. "Good," he said. "Because you'll need all your strength today. Stick together as a team and you'll be all right."

Ha! I thought. *That isn't very likely.*

As I left the food tent shortly afterwards, I was still feeling fed up. But fortunately something happened just then to make me feel a bit happier. The rain had stopped, and as we waited to start the day's walk, the sun came out and suddenly there was the most amazing view of the clouds below us. I had only ever seen that view from a plane window before, and it was truly beautiful.

Unfortunately, the view of the clouds was the best thing about the day. Gunter hadn't been lying when he had said we would need all our strength. Nobody talked much. We needed all our energy to walk. And my feet were really hurting again.

When we stopped for lunch, I started to take my boots off to look at my feet. And that's when I noticed that my boots were damaged. I hadn't bought new walking boots for the trip because I'd thought it was best to walk in a pair of old, comfortable boots. But obviously my boots were a little too old. And they certainly weren't comfortable any longer.

I stared down at the damage, feeling really shocked. The top of my right boot was coming right away from the bottom! And the left boot wasn't much better. Suddenly, I saw Gunter walking around the group, checking to see if everyone was OK. He mustn't see! Quickly I put my boots back on. They had to be OK. If they weren't, Gunter would send me back down the mountain! I couldn't fail this challenge because of a stupid mistake with my boots. I just couldn't!

Gunter had reached me now. "All right, Alison?" he asked.

I stood up and smiled brightly. "Yes, I'm fine, thanks, Gunter. I'm ready to go on."

And that's why my feet hurt so much when we finally reached the next camp just before it got dark.

Fortunately, Kelly had concerns of her own when we washed in the tent before dinner, so she didn't notice the look of pain on my face when I took my socks off.

"I think I'm coming down with a cold!" she said, blowing her nose.

"Oh, poor you," I said.

"Yes, it must be because of getting so wet the other day. I hope it doesn't get any worse! They don't let you carry on if you get a bad cold, you know. It's too dangerous at altitude."

After dinner, Gunter got to his feet. "OK, everyone," he said, "I just wanted to tell you something about tomorrow. We'll be climbing the Barranco Wall, which is 300 meters high. It looks difficult, but it's not so bad really. Most people really enjoy it. It's a good challenge."

"Will we be using climbing equipment?" someone asked.

"No," Gunter answered. "We won't need anything like that. There is a sort of path, and you'll be stepping from rock to rock. You'll need to concentrate hard and to look carefully for safe places to put your hands and your feet. But you'll be fine. The guides will be there to help you. Let's hope the weather is good."

But the weather wasn't good. And now I had Kelly's cold. I didn't feel too great at all.

It was still raining when we set off. I had my head down to keep the rain from my face. When I looked up, the Barranco Wall was straight ahead, a large wall of rock with its top disappearing into the heavy rain clouds.

We all stood and looked up at it. I don't think I was the only one who was feeling afraid.

Will I really be able to get to the top? I thought.

There was only one way to find out.

"You must take extra care today," Gunter told us all before we began to climb. "The rocks will be slippery because of the rain. And remember what I said, you must concentrate on what you're doing. Look very carefully where you are putting your hands and your feet."

The previous evening, Gunter had said there was a "sort of path" up the Barranco Wall. As we began to make our way up, I didn't think that "path" was the right word. You could certainly see where others had gone up, but it wasn't exactly a path. A lot of the time we were pulling ourselves up from rock to rock. Sometimes we had to sit down and slide. Often the space was so narrow we had to turn toward the rock as we walked slowly along. When the porters wanted to get by, we had to hold on tight and stand still.

The Barranco Wall was crowded. Ours wasn't the only group climbing up that day; there were lots of other groups as well and progress was slow. Soon it was very busy indeed. A long line of people were making their way carefully up the Wall, taking one step, then waiting, taking another step, then waiting. We were very close to each other. Too close. More than once, stones rolled down the path toward me as the people in front made their way up. Gunter had been right. We did need all our concentration.

Unfortunately, for me, concentrating was the hardest thing of all. My feet were really hurting by now, and my cold was making me feel really bad. But even worse than that, I just couldn't stop thinking about my problems at home and the decisions I had to make. I suppose the conversation I'd had with Harvey the previous evening was still running around in my head. I kept on imagining house hunting with Dad. And then there was the thought of starting back at work for a new term.

If I didn't buy a house near the college, then I'd have to travel for a long time to get to work. Was that what I wanted from my life? To have to travel across a busy city just to get to a job I didn't enjoy? Because if I had the responsibility of owning a house and paying money back to

the bank, then I would need to keep my secure job as a teacher. And I really wasn't sure I wanted to carry on being a teacher. I had allowed Dad to make me think that being an art teacher was the only job I could do, but was that really true? Would it really be so impossible for me to make a living just from my paintings? Could I be an artist?

It all happened so quickly. The girl in front of me had gone on ahead. I hadn't been watching to see where she'd put her hands and her feet, and I didn't take enough time to choose where to put mine. I put all my weight on a broken piece of rock, and immediately my foot started to slide from under me. Before I knew it, I was falling.

Chapter 7

A fall

I screamed out, trying to get hold of something, anything, to stop myself from falling. But it was no good. My shoulder made painful contact with a rock as I fell from the path, almost taking the girl behind with me. Rocks began to fall around me. I heard someone call out my name. I fell and fell and fell. Then finally I hit the ground hard and stopped.

I lay there with my eyes closed for what seemed like a long time. Around me there was silence, and the only thing I felt was an awful pain in my shoulder. Then, "Alison?" Suddenly I could hear a voice from a long way away. There was something wet on my face. I tried to move, but pain shot through my shoulder, and I lay still again.

I opened my eyes. It was raining hard.

"Don't move, Alison," called a voice—Gunter. "We're coming down to you."

"Alison!" called another voice. "Are you OK?" It was Bill.

"I . . . I think so," I said. I could feel pain in other parts of my body now, my back and my legs and my head. Probably from where I'd hit the rocks on my way down. There was a strange taste in my mouth, too, and I wondered if it was blood. Perhaps the wetness on my face wasn't just the rain.

I wanted to try and move again, but there was something stopping me, something heavy. I felt myself shaking with shock and cold. Why hadn't I taken more care where I had

put my feet? If this meant I had to go back down the mountain without trying for the summit, then I would have let everyone down. Now, because of me, Susie wouldn't get enough money for her operation. I couldn't bear it.

It seemed like forever that I just lay there, waiting for someone to reach me. I thought about Gill and wished with all my heart that she were there with me. But she wasn't, and I couldn't even hear her voice in my head anymore. She was gone . . . gone. And I had never felt so completely alone in all my life.

"Alison?" I opened my eyes. It was Gunter with Roger, the trip doctor. Bill wasn't far behind. I looked to see if Harvey was there, too, but I couldn't see him.

"I'm just going to take these rocks off you," Gunter said. "Don't worry, you'll be all right."

The weight holding me down was suddenly gone. I tried to move, but the doctor pushed me gently back. "Not yet. Let's just check you out first." He was looking at my head carefully. "You have a cut on your face," he said. "But I don't think it's very deep. Did you hit your head?"

"I don't think so," I answered, but the doctor looked anyway.

"That all looks OK," he said.

He took a look at my shoulder then asked me questions about what else hurt and made me move my hands, arms, and legs.

Bill and Kelly were nearby the whole time the doctor was working on me. Gunter was there too.

"What happened, Alison?" Kelly asked. "Do you know?"

"There . . . there was a loose rock," I said. "When I stepped on it, I started to slide."

"Can you try and sit up now, Alison?" the doctor was asking me, and with his help, I managed to do it. My shoulder really hurt.

"You were very lucky, Alison," the doctor said to me. "You don't seem to have broken anything. But you are going to feel a bit uncomfortable for a while."

Then Gunter noticed my boots. "Your boots can't have helped," he said. "They're in a terrible state!"

We all looked at them. They were well and truly finished.

"I think," said Gunter, looking over, "that you may be going down the mountain, Alison."

The tears came right back again as I saw Bill and Kelly both trying to hide their feelings from me. I couldn't let everybody down. I just couldn't!

"No!" I said to Gunter. "I can't do that! I have to carry on. Please! I've only hurt my shoulder. I don't need my shoulder to walk."

"But I don't see how you can continue walking with those boots," Gunter said. "It's too dangerous."

"Please, Gunter!" I said.

Bill spoke to Gunter. "Look," he said, "why don't we just help Alison to the top of the Wall, Gunter? I'm sure we'll be able to sort something out. Someone might have a second pair of boots that she could use."

The accident had brought everything to a stop on the Barranco Wall. By this time there was a very long line of people behind us, waiting to continue up to the top.

Gunter made a decision. "OK," he agreed. "Do you think you can carry on to the top, if we help you, Alison? We'll have our lunch up there and then we'll decide what to do."

"Oh, yes!" I said. "I'm sure I can."

"We'll all help!" said Kelly.

And they did. Matt carried my bag, and Bill and Gunter took it in turns to support me to the top. I needed their support. I hadn't hurt my legs, but they didn't feel very strong. I suppose it was because of the shock of the fall. As for Kelly, she gave me encouragement the whole time. "You can do it, Alison!" "Not far now!" "I can see the top!"

Until finally, we were there.

"We'll have lunch here," Gunter announced, and everyone was happy to sit down and take a rest.

I took my boots off, and when Roger came over to check on me, he saw my feet.

They looked as terrible as they felt, and I wasn't surprised when he drew in a breath. "Your feet look really painful, Alison," he said. "How long have they been like this?" He looked up at me just as I had to blow my nose, and I saw him notice my red eyes. "And you've got a cold too, haven't you?" he said.

"Not really," I said quickly. "Well, only a slight one. Look, can you do anything for my feet?"

There was doubt on the doctor's face. "I can try," he said.

He tried, and it hurt. A lot. And all the time he was working on my feet, I was thinking about how good everyone had been to me. For the whole of the trip I'd been doing my best to believe I didn't need anybody. Now I knew that wasn't true. I would never have gotten to the top of the Barranco Wall without them all.

Chapter 8

A big decision

The doctor had finished with me. I knew Gunter would be over any moment. I could see Harvey in the distance, sitting on a rock. I felt hurt that he hadn't come over to see if I was all right. Surely he had known about my fall when we were still on the Barranco Wall? Why hadn't he come to help? I'd thought we were friends.

I didn't want to go over to him. I felt a bit upset about his behavior. But Harvey was very experienced and practical and I knew he might be able to think of a way to help. If I didn't want to go down the mountain, I had to try everything. So I went over. My feet weren't so painful now, but I knew they were likely to start hurting again if I wore my old boots to walk in.

As I approached, I saw that Harvey's eyes were closed. His lunch lay untouched, beside him. "Harvey?"

When he opened his eyes to look at me, I remembered how his eyes had seemed unfocused the other evening at dinner. They still looked that way. "Alison," he said. "Are you OK? I didn't come down to help; there already seemed to be too many people down there with you. I didn't want to get in the way."

Part of me still felt hurt by this, but another part of me was concerned because Harvey's voice didn't sound right, and it wasn't like him not to eat his food. "I'm fine," I said. "Well, I hurt my shoulder a little, but I'm OK. But how are you?

You seem . . . well, you don't seem like yourself."

"Of course, I am," he said. "I'm just preparing myself for the next stage of the walk. Having some quiet time."

Once again, his voice sounded strange, as if he were really tired. "You haven't eaten anything," I said.

"I'm not hungry," he answered and then he paused, as if he were waiting for me to say what I'd come for. He seemed distant, almost as if all our happy conversations had never taken place.

"My boots have fallen apart," I told him, still looking at his face. "I may have to go down the mountain." I couldn't keep the emotion out of my voice. As I said it, it seemed like a real possibility. And I had never wanted to get to the top more than I did at that moment. For Susie and for me, I wanted to succeed.

Harvey took a while to answer. Then he looked at my boots. "I might be able to help you there," he said finally, still in that strange voice, and he began to look through his backpack.

As he took things out and laid them on the ground, it seemed to take a huge amount of effort. I was certain something was wrong.

"Harvey," I said, "I don't think you're well. I think you should speak to Gunter."

"I'm fine, Alison," he said and now he sounded a bit angry with me.

I just stood there staring at him worriedly as he kept on looking through his bag. Finally, he found what he was looking for and pulled it out.

As he held it up, I saw that it was a reel of strong, black

tape. "This might help," he said and he handed the tape to me.

I reached out to take it. "Thanks," I said, but I didn't move away. Harvey had his eyes closed again. This was more than just tiredness. He had altitude sickness; I knew it. "Please, Harvey," I said, "speak to Gunter. If you've got bad altitude sickness and you carry on walking, it could be dangerous for you."

Harvey opened his eyes again. This time he looked really angry with me. "Just leave it, Alison, OK? *I came here to climb this mountain, and that's what I'm going to do. I'm a big boy. I can take care of myself. I suggest you concentrate on sorting out your own problems!*" Then he started to put his things back into his backpack.

I was still standing there feeling shocked and hurt when Bill came over. He saw the tape. "Hey," he said. "That's just the job! Get your boots off, Alison, and let's give it a go!"

I took my boots off and Bill proceeded to use the tape on them. When I looked up again, Harvey had gone. I looked around for him, worriedly. I didn't know what to do. It hurt that Harvey had been so angry with me. But that could just be part of his sickness.

Bill had finished with one of my boots. "Here," he said. "Try this on; see how it feels."

So I tried the boot on, and then the other one after Bill had finished with it. Then Gunter came over and I had to make him believe that they were fine and my feet didn't hurt any longer and I was quite all right to continue with the walk.

"OK," Gunter said at last. "You can walk to the next camp, and we'll see how your feet are then."

I was so pleased I kissed him. Bill laughed. Even Matt smiled.

But then, during the four-hour walk to camp, I returned to worrying about Harvey. I still hadn't made up my mind what I was going to do about him by the time we had dinner.

I saw him sitting alone at the end of the table. He didn't appear to be eating very much. I was surer than ever that something was wrong. I was just going to mention it to Bill when Gunter got to his feet to talk about the climb to the summit.

"Tomorrow will be very hard," he said, "possibly the hardest thing many of you have ever done in your lives. We will walk for five hours until we reach Barafu Ridge Camp. Then we will eat dinner and you will go to bed at six o'clock in the evening." He looked around at us and smiled. "The view from the summit is nearly always best early in the morning when the sun comes up, so for that reason we are going to walk through the night. You must try to sleep this evening so that when you wake, your body will think it is the next day."

It sounded simple, but when I looked at Kelly I knew she was thinking the same thing as I was. *Will I be able to sleep?*

Gunter was continuing. "At eleven o'clock tomorrow evening, the porters will wake you. Around midnight, we will start out for the summit. We will walk all night, and soon after dawn we will reach Stella Point. From Stella Point, it is another hour's walk to Uhuru Peak, which is the top of the mountain. Now, does anybody have any questions?"

"Yes," said Bill. "Have you got any porters available to carry me up to the top?"

Everybody laughed. I smiled. A few days previously, I might not have found it funny. But now I knew that there was a whole lot more to Bill than just making jokes.

He had been really good to me.

Opposite me, Kelly didn't look at all well. I had a cold too, but it was nothing like Kelly's.

"Are you all right?" I asked Kelly as she blew her nose again.

"Yes," Kelly said. "I just need to get to bed. Sleep this off. I'll be fine for tomorrow." It was almost as if she was saying it to make herself believe it.

"Think she'll make it?" Matt asked Bill after Kelly had left.

"She'll try her best," said Bill. "She's made of pretty strong stuff."

Matt looked doubtful. "We'll see," he said, and then he got up. "Good night all."

"I'm coming too," Bill started to say, but I put out a hand to stop him.

"Before you go, Bill . . ." I said.

He sat down again, looking at me, and I felt my face grow warm. "I just want to say . . . thank you for today."

Bill put up a hand. "You don't have to thank me," he said. "We're a team, aren't we? We look out for each other."

"But I haven't been really," I said. "Part of the team. Not up until now. And you . . . well, I wouldn't have made it without you today. So . . . thank you."

"Hey," Bill said kindly, taking my hand. "It hasn't been easy, has it? But you're made of strong stuff, too."

Gunter came over. "Let's take a look at your boots, Alison," he said.

He looked at them carefully, and then stood up again. "You did a good job, my friend," he said to Bill. "I think you'll be all right, Alison. Now, both of you, get some sleep."

Across the room, I saw Harvey leaving the food tent. "I just want a quick word with Harvey," I told Bill. "Good night."

"Good night, Alison," Bill said with a smile.

I reached Harvey just as he was about to enter his tent. "Harvey?" I said, and he looked round at me. It was too dark to see him very well, but I could see he was holding one hand to his head as if it was hurting.

He didn't seem to recognize me at first. "Yes?" he said. Then he said, "Oh, Alison. I'm . . . just going to bed."

"I won't keep you," I said. "I just wanted to say thank you. For the tape."

For a moment, he didn't look as if he knew what I meant. "The tape," he repeated. Once again his voice sounded odd. He hadn't taken his hand away from his head, and as I watched, he closed his eyes for a moment. It was obvious that he had a really bad headache.

"For . . . my boots," I reminded him softly.

"Oh," he said. "Yes. Good. Well, good night."

"Good night, Harvey." As he started to go into his tent, he almost fell. It was all I needed to make up my mind.

Chapter 9

Summit night

As I walked up to Gunter, I couldn't forget the look in Harvey's eyes, or the tone of his voice earlier. *"I came here to climb this mountain, and that's what I'm going to do! I suggest you concentrate on sorting out your own problems!"* It was the same way my boss, David Spence, spoke to me, and my dad too, sometimes. Usually I shut up if someone spoke like that, but not this time. I just couldn't let Harvey take this risk. The doctor would know what to do.

"Gunter," I said, "could I talk to you for a moment, please?"

He looked at my serious expression. "Of course," he said. "Let's go into the food tent."

I followed him and we sat down. "What is it, Alison?" he asked. "Are you worried about tomorrow? Nobody will think you are a failure if you decide not to go ahead."

I shook my head. "No," I said. "This isn't about me. It . . . it's about Harvey."

"Harvey?" Gunter looked surprised.

"Yes," I said. "I think he's ill. I think he's got altitude sickness. He didn't want me to say anything to you, but . . . well, I think maybe you and Roger should take a look yourself. I'm worried about him."

Just at that moment, Roger came into the tent and Gunter called him over.

I told them both what I'd noticed. "I think he's in a lot of pain, and his voice sounds strange. He nearly fell just now, too."

"Thank you, Alison," Roger said. "We'll go and check it out."

They walked quickly away. I went back to my tent. Kelly was in there. She could tell immediately that something was wrong.

"What is it?" she asked.

"I think Harvey's very ill," I told her. "I've just told Gunter and Roger. They've gone to see him."

"Oh," said Kelly. "I see. I'm sorry." She looked at me. "You like him, don't you?"

"Yes," I agreed. "I do. He's easy to talk to. At least, he usually is. That's what made me think something was wrong. He changed. Suddenly he seemed cross with me all the time."

Perhaps Kelly could hear the hurt in my voice, because she took my hand.

We sat together and listened. It wasn't difficult to hear. Harvey's tent wasn't very far away from ours, and Harvey spoke loudly.

"It's Alison, isn't it?" he said. "She's come running to you with some story about me being ill! Well, it's not true. I'm fine!"

But he didn't *sound* fine.

Gunter came and found me later. He told me that Roger had confirmed my opinion. Harvey had bad altitude sickness and he needed to go down the mountain. He would not be trying for the summit.

Even though I knew I'd done the right thing, I still felt terrible. Getting to the summit had been so important to Harvey. I shall never forget the look in his eyes as he was led away by a guide the next morning. He looked at me as if he absolutely hated me, and I knew it was the last time I would ever see him.

As I stared unhappily after him, I felt a hand on my arm. It was Bill. Kelly and Matt were with him. Everyone was standing around talking. The news had spread.

"You did the right thing, Alison," Bill told me.

"I know," I said. "It just doesn't feel like it somehow."

"Someone like Harvey is so set on achieving something, they ignore the warning signs," Matt said. He shook his head. "I should know. It's exactly what I did with my leg. If I'd only followed expert advice, I might still be playing professional rugby today."

I looked at him, aware that it had probably cost him a lot to make such an admission. I thought he had probably suffered quite a lot over the loss of his career. Teaching was a second choice for him, too.

"It was very brave of you to speak up, Alison," Kelly was saying, and I had to agree.

"Yes," I said. "It felt brave. I knew how much Harvey wanted to get to the top. And I . . . well, sometimes I let people push me around too much. Gill was always encouraging me to speak out more. This time . . . well, I just had to. I couldn't risk someone else dying."

We all stood quietly, thinking about Gill.

When we went into the food tent, none of us felt like eating very much. We had a very long day ahead of us, the most important day of the trip. But somehow it just seemed wrong to be preparing to set off for the day's walk to the final camp as if nothing had happened. But we had to. Harvey might be gone, but Susie still needed us.

As we walked tiredly into the final camp six hours later, the porters all sang a song of welcome to us that made us smile. By five o'clock we were all in our tents. I'm not sure if I slept or not. A little, possibly. It only seemed like five minutes before a porter was calling into our tent.

"Eleven o'clock, ladies, time to get up."

Silently, Kelly and I got dressed in our warmest clothes. Then, when we were ready, Kelly touched my arm. "All right?" she asked.

I gave her a smile and put on my gloves. "Yes," I said. "I'm all right."

We left the tent and went out into the dark. Bill was standing with Matt. When he saw us, Bill smiled and opened his arms. We went into them and soon Matt was there too, and we were having a group hug. I was way beyond feeling tired. I had absolutely no idea how I was going to make it to the top of the mountain. I only knew I was going to make it. We all were. We were a group, a team, and we were going to succeed together.

It was sad that now I had finally let these people get close to me, I was going to have to leave them. But I did have to leave them. I had spoken up about Harvey, and now I had to speak out about what I wanted for my future. I had to speak up for myself. I was going to refuse Dad's offer. I had to.

I turned to Kelly. I wanted to share my decision with somebody.

"When this is all over," I said, "I'm going to give up teaching. I'm going to be a full-time artist. It's what I've always wanted."

Kelly looked at me. "Really?" she said.

I smiled. "Really."

"Well," she said. "We'll miss you. But if that's what you really want, then you should do it."

I smiled at her. "I'm going to."

Then Gunter was calling, "Good luck, everybody!" and there was no more time for talking.

I don't remember very much about the first few hours of the walk. It was unbelievably hard, walking through the dark when I was already so tired, and when there just didn't seem to be enough air to breathe because of the altitude. The only thing I can remember clearly are the lights above me. At first I thought they were stars, but then I realized they were the head torches of the people in front, going slowly, slowly, up the mountain.

Lift one foot. Place it in front of the other. Push down. Breathe and rest. Lift the other foot. Place it in front of the other. Push down. Breathe and rest. Repeat. Every step was a fight, a fight between ourselves and the mountain. There was almost total silence except for breathing. Nobody had the energy to talk.

And then, suddenly, the sun rose. It was beautiful, but it would have been more beautiful without the slight fog that was hanging around, spoiling the view. We could still see quite a distance, but not as far as we'd like to.

Someone was nearby. It was Matt. "Look," he said. "There's Stella Point, just up there." He talked slowly with a great effort, but I looked up at the place where Gunter had told us we were going to rest briefly before we made our final push for the summit. It didn't look too far away. About fifteen minutes.

It took another hour. I was so happy to get there, to be walking through the snow, with only another hour to walk to get to the top of the mountain. I was too tired to care about the fog that meant we couldn't see very far. But I *did* care that there was no sign of Bill and Kelly, and I looked around worriedly for them. Gunter had told us we mustn't stay long at Stella Point, or we would get too cold to continue. Lots of people, he had told us, had got this far and then had to turn back without reaching the summit. To have come so far and suffered so much and then to fail! That just *couldn't* happen.

But for Matt and I to go up to the top without the others? I didn't want to do that either.

"I think I can see them!" Matt told me, and when I looked, I saw that he was right. There was Bill's red and yellow hat, and there was Kelly beside him. There were tears in my eyes when they finally made it.

Bill and Kelly only had time for a few minutes' rest before we had to set off again. I was so impressed by the way they just accepted the situation and got on with it. If I ever met their children, I wanted to try to tell them what heroes their parents were.

We had to rest a lot. All of us felt sick. It was like walking in a dream, a bad dream where you keep on moving but you're actually stuck in one place. What we were forcing our bodies to do seemed impossible, and yet somehow we did it. Slowly. Weakly. On, rest. On, rest. On . . . All the time going up a little more. Ever a little closer to our goal.

And then at last we were there, standing on the roof of Africa. The summit of Kilimanjaro. We screamed, we shouted, and we put our arms around each other. And last, we cried.

The fog had lifted, and there were clouds and mountaintops as far as we could see.

"It's so beautiful!" Kelly breathed, and it was true. It was.

"I think she's here with us," I said tearfully. "Gill . . . I can feel her."

We all still had our arms around each other. "Me too," said Matt.

There was the sound of happy laughter as other people reached the summit.

"It was Gill who made the fog go away!" Kelly said, and I smiled at the thought.

"Yes," I agreed. "She'd do that for us, wouldn't she?"

"Oh, she would," agreed Bill. "She would."

Bill did a bit of filming, and then he turned the camera off, and we just stood there, the four of us, our arms around each other, looking out at the sun playing on the snow and the rocks and the huge blue sky. We knew that now we could pay for Susie to have her operation in America, and we were so happy about that we were crying and smiling at the same time.

Someone took this photo of us. I'll keep it forever. It's proof that I can achieve amazing things, both on my own and with other people. And when I look at it, it will also remind me of the time that I found the confidence to speak out, to voice my opinion when I knew I was right.

And the time when I made the decision to do what I really wanted to do with my life.

Before we left the summit, I heard Gill's voice one last time. *"Well done, Alison! Well done!"*

"Last one down gets to pay for dinner!" joked Bill, and we all smiled and started back down the mountain together.

Review: Chapters 1–5

A. Number these events in the order that they happened (1–7).

_____ Alison tells Kelly she uses her phone too much.

_____ The group meets Harvey for the first time.

_____ Alison sees thousands of stars in the sky.

_____ It is foggy on the walk to Shira Cathedral.

__1__ The group has a meal in Arusha, Tanzania.

_____ Alison sees balloons put up by Kelly in the tent.

_____ The climb begins.

B. Read each statement and circle whether it is true (T) or false (F).

1. Alison was Gill's best friend.   T / F

2. Harvey is climbing Kilimanjaro to raise money for his   T / F

   daughter's operation.

3. At the start of the climb, the group carry their own backpacks.   T / F

4. Alison and Kelly are sharing a tent.   T / F

5. Bill's son is a teenager.   T / F

C. Circle the correct word or phrase in italics to complete each sentence.

1. Bill is making a *film / painting* of the climb.

2. The *porters / group* carry their big bags up the mountain.

3. Alison thinks Matt's jokes are *funny / not funny*.

4. Alison's *father / mother* wants to help her to buy a house.

5. Gunter tells Alison to walk *quickly / slowly* on the way to Shira Cathedral.

6. Kelly's *sister / mother* is looking after her son.

D. Choose the best answer for each question.

1. Kelly is worried about her son because he _____.

  a. is playful

  b. doesn't have good manners

  c. is not healthy

2. Matt thinks the others will struggle to get to the summit because they _____.

  a. don't know each other well

  b. didn't prepare properly

  c. don't work well with each other

3. The group is climbing Kilimanjaro to raise money _____.

  a. for Gill's daughter

  b. for the company

  c. to build a hospital

4. Harvey says Alison likes to be _____.

  a. sad

  b. alone

  c. grumpy

Review: Chapters 6–9

A. Complete each sentence using the correct name from the box. Two names are extra.

| Alison | Harvey | Gunter | Matt | Bill | Kelly |

1. _____ says they will need to concentrate when they are climbing the Barranco Wall.

2. _____ has some tape to mend Alison's boots.

3. _____ has a bad cold.

4. _____ carries Alison's backpack.

B. Read each statement and circle whether it is true (T) or false (F).

1. It is raining when the group climbs the Barranco Wall. T / F

2. Bill's boots fall apart. T / F

3. Kelly gets altitude sickness. T / F

4. Alison speaks to Gunter about Harvey. T / F

5. Harvey gets to the top of the mountain. T / F

C. Complete the crossword puzzle using the clues below.

Across
3. Kelly isn't feeling well. She has a _____.
5. Alison uses Harvey's _____ to mend her boots.
7. The rocks on the Barranco Wall are _____.

Down
1. _____ is the trip doctor.
2. The weather is _____ when the group climbs the Barranco Wall.
4. Alison is worried about the damage to her _____.
6. Harvey is _____ because Alison spoke to Gunter about his health.

D. Choose the best answer for each question.

1. Alison's boots were damaged because _____ .

   a. they got wet

   b. someone stepped on them

   c. they were old

2. The group used _____ to climb the Barranco Wall.

   a. climbing equipment

   b. their hands and feet

   c. animals of labor

3. When Alison slipped and fell, she cut her _____ .

   a. hands

   b. face

   c. legs

4. Harvey didn't make it to the summit because he had _____ .

   a. a bad cold

   b. a stomach ache

   c. altitude sickness

Answer Key

Chapters 1–5

A:
5, 2, 4, 7, 1, 6, 3

B:
1. T; **2.** F; **3.** T; **4.** T; **5.** F

C:
1. film; **2.** porters; **3.** not funny; **4.** father; **5.** slowly; **6.** mother

D:
1. c; **2.** b; **3.** a; **4.** b

Chapters 6–9

A:
1. Gunter; **2.** Harvey; **3.** Kelly; **4.** Matt

B:
1. T; **2.** F; **3.** F; **4.** T; **5.** F

C:
Across:
3. cold; **5.** tape; **7.** slippery

Down:
1. Roger; **2.** wet; **4.** boots; **6.** angry

D:
1. c; **2.** b; **3.** b; **4.** c

Background Reading:

Spotlight on . . . *Mount Kilimanjaro*

In 1889, Hans Meyer and Ludwig Purtscheller became the first Europeans to climb Mount Kilimanjaro, Africa's highest mountain. Today, about 15,000 people attempt to climb the mountain every year. They do this as a spiritual journey, a personal challenge, or to help to raise money for charity.

Mount Kilimanjaro rises to 5,895 meters and comprises three volcanoes: Kibo, Mawenzi, and Shira. Shira and Mawenzi are extinct, but Kibo is dormant—it last erupted over 150,000 years ago. Kilimanjaro has varied forest types and natural features. Someone climbing the mountain will pass through rain forest, moorland, alpine desert, and glaciers. Animals such as elephants, buffaloes, monkeys, and mountain hawks can be seen in many parts of the mountain, except close to the summit.

Nobody is completely sure how Mount Kilimanjaro got its name. Most people think it comes from the Swahili words *kilimanjaro*, meaning "shining mountain." People living close to the mountain believed that the shiny snow on its peak was evidence that evil spirits guarded the mountain. People who attempted to climb the mountain disappeared or returned with horrible injuries caused by the severe cold.

Today, of the 15,000 people who attempt to climb the mountain each year, only about 40 percent reach Uhuru Peak, the summit. The majority are forced to turn back at Gilman's Point, 300 meters from Uhuru Peak, or at Stella Point, which is 200 meters from Uhuru. Most give up because of altitude sickness. Each year there are also deaths on the mountain, mostly due to hypothermia—a condition where the body's temperature falls below the usual level. It is usually caused by being in the severe cold for a long time.

Think About It

1. Why do you think so many people climb Mount Kilimanjaro every year?
2. Do you think climbing Mount Kilimanjaro would be dangerous? Would you do it?

Spotlight on . . . *Mountain survival*

Mountains can be dangerous places. It is important to prepare and plan before you set off, to prevent getting hurt or lost. Here are some tips to keep in mind.

Mountaineering skills and equipment

- Learn basic mountaineering skills, such as reading a map and using a compass.
- Learn how to do some basic first aid, for example, CPR ("the kiss of life") and treating hypothermia (very low body temperature).

The right equipment

- The right equipment is important—a map and compass are essential, and a GPS device can be very useful. A cell phone is useful, but some mountain areas have no phone signal. A whistle is useful for signaling your position to rescuers if you are lost. A flashlight (plus spare batteries and bulbs) is also very important. If you need to signal for help, turn it on and off six times, then stop for a minute. Repeat.

Suitable clothing and footwear

- Choose suitable footwear which provides support for your ankles.
- Clothing should be colorful, warm, windproof, and waterproof. You should always carry spare clothing in case the temperature changes, even in summer.

Carry food and drink

- Take plenty of food and drink. High-energy food, such as chocolate and dried fruit, is ideal.
- In cold, wet weather, a warm drink is advisable where possible. Always carry water, even in cool weather.

Keep an eye on the weather and its effect on the body

- Keep an eye on the weather and be prepared to turn back if the weather gets bad, even if this upsets a long-planned adventure.
- Watch for signs of hypothermia, particularly in bad weather. Look out for confusion, shivering and appearing cold, tiredness, a pale face, not being able to feel hands or toes, or when people take off clothing they should be wearing.

Think About It

1. If you were lost on a mountain, what would you do?
2. What other equipment and skills do you think a mountain climber needs? Make a list.

Glossary

altitude	(*n.*)	the height of something above sea level or above the earth's surface
backpack	(*n.*)	a bag carried on the back, often while hiking
camp	(*n.*)	a place where walkers or mountaineers rest
colleague	(*n.*)	a person you work with
concentrate	(*v.*)	to think carefully and deeply
counselor	(*n.*)	a person who gives other people advice and support, often in a college or school
head torch	(*n.*)	a special light worn on the head
porter	(*n.*)	a person who helps to carry things
professionally	(*adv.*)	in a joblike manner
rugby	(*n.*)	a team sport played with an oval ball
sketchbook	(*n.*)	a book that you can draw in
slide	(*v.*)	to move down something quickly; slip
snore (snoring)	(*v.*)	to make a noise when you sleep
summit	(*n.*)	the top of the mountain
tent	(*n.*)	a temporary shelter, often used on walking trips

NOTES

NOTES

DATE DUE	RETURNED